Joseph in Egypt

Joseph came from Canaan. His brothers hated him and they sold him as a slave to an Egyptian. He worked hard for his master, Potiphar, and became head of his household.

Potiphar's wife told lies about Joseph and he was thrown into prison. There, he met two of Pharaoh's servants. One night they each had a dream and asked Joseph what they meant. God helped Joseph to understand the dreams and he told the men the meanings. He said one of the men would be set free and the other would be hanged. The dreams came true.

Some time later Pharaoh had a dream. He watched seven fat cows come out of the river. Seven thin cows followed. The seven thin cows ate the seven fat cows. Pharaoh then dreamt of seven thin ears of corn eating up seven plump ears of corn. He was puzzled. No one could tell him what the dreams meant.

Eventually, Pharaoh heard about Joseph's skill of understanding dreams and Joseph was brought out of prison. He told Pharaoh what the dreams meant. Egypt would have seven years of rich harvest followed by seven years of famine. He told Pharaoh that in the good years the grain should be saved. They would then have enough to eat when the famine came.

Pharaoh was very pleased with Joseph and he made him a ruler over all Egypt. The good years came and the grain was stored. Then the famine came.

Back in Canaan, Joseph's father, Jacob, sent his sons to Egypt to buy corn for his people. But he did not send his youngest son, Benjamin. When the sons came to Joseph they did not recognise him in his fine clothes as ruler over Egypt. Joseph knew who they were. He sold them some corn but demanded that they return with Benjamin. He had one of his brothers bound and put in prison until they returned.

Twice, Joseph played a trick on his brothers. First, he gave them back their money by hiding it in one of the sacks of corn. Then, he hid his silver cup with the corn. When the brothers discovered the money and the cup they were frightened. They thought they would be accused of stealing. They went back to Joseph. This time he told his brothers who he really was. They were full of joy and returned to Jacob in Canaan to tell him the good news. Jacob agreed to return to Egypt with his sons and their families. They made their home there, and lived as shepherds in Goshen.

You can find this story in Genesis chapters 39-47.

Samuel in the Temple

Elkanah had two wives, Hannah and Peninnah. Hannah had no children, but Peninnah did have some, and she often laughed at Hannah because of this.

Every year Elkanah and his family went to Shiloh to worship God at the temple. Hannah was sad, and she went to the temple to pray. The priest, Eli, saw her and spoke kindly to her. He trusted that God would answer Hannah's prayer. She had been asking God that she might have a baby son. She promised that she would give her child to serve God.

They all went back home, and after some time Hannah's prayer was indeed answered. She had a baby son. Hannah was very happy. She named the baby Samuel because the name means, 'I ask God for him'.

After some time had passed, Hannah remembered the promise she had made to God. She took Samuel to the temple and gave him to Eli the priest. Samuel would help Eli in the temple. Every year Hannah visited Samuel and each time she took him a new little coat.

Samuel grew to love God more, and the people loved Samuel too. Eli had two sons, but they behaved wickedly and were not fit to be priests.

Eli was now quite old and almost blind. One night, when they had both gone to bed, something very wonderful happened. Samuel slept near the Ark of the Covenant and he was awakened by a voice saying,
"Samuel, Samuel".
He ran to Eli and asked what he wanted. Eli replied that he had not called for Samuel.
Again, the voice called Samuel, and again he went to Eli.

The third time that the voice called, Eli realised it was God speaking to Samuel.
He told Samuel to go back to bed, and if God were to speak again, he should listen to what God had to say.

Samuel did this and listened carefully to what God said. He told Samuel that he was very angry with the sons of Eli, and also with Eli, because he did not stop his sons from being wicked. Samuel went to tell Eli. God would do whatever was the right thing, and Eli accepted this.

The people listened to Samuel when he told them God's messages. They knew he was a great helper of God.

You can find this story in I Samuel chapters 1-3.

The Tabernacle in the Wilderness

STORY 3

Moses was the great leader of the Israelites. He had led them out of Egypt where they had been slaves. They had crossed the Red Sea and arrived in the wilderness of the Sinai Desert. They were on their way to the promised land.

God cared for them in the desert and they eventually arrived at the foot of Mount Sinai.

Moses told them he was going up the mountain to speak with God. While he was up the mountain, God gave Moses the ten commandments written on two stone tablets, and many other laws to guide the people to live as God wanted.

God also told Moses to tell the Israelites to build a portable temple, called the tabernacle, which they could take with them as they travelled. Moses was up the mountain for forty days and forty nights.

It was a long time for Moses to be away and the people got restless. They wanted to worship a god they could see. Aaron, who was in charge whilst Moses was away, allowed them to melt down golden jewellery and they moulded a great golden calf. They danced around the calf and prayed to it. They got drunk and behaved wildly. Moses was angry when he saw them and threw the stone tablets to the ground. He asked God to forgive the people.

They started to work on building the Tabernacle. This was a tent fourteen metres long by five metres high and four metres wide. In it was placed the Ark; a golden box in which the ten commandments on new stone tablets were kept. There were two rooms in the Tabernacle. The Ark was in the smaller one, called the Holy of Holies. The other room had a bronze altar, a seven-branched candlestick and a gold table on which twelve loaves of bread were placed.

The Tabernacle was positioned in a courtyard surrounded by walls. All the people were allowed to pray in the courtyard, but only the High Priest was allowed in the Holy of Holies. In the courtyard was a large altar and a bronze bowl for washing hands.

By day, the Tabernacle was covered with a cloud. This meant that God's presence was there. When the cloud lifted and moved, the people followed it and continued their journey. At night, there was a fire in the cloud so everybody could see it.

The Israelites now had a Tabernacle with them where they could worship God wherever they went. God led his people towards the Promised Land.

You can find this story in Exodus chapters 19-40.

The Walls Came Tumbling Down

STORY 4

Joshua was now the leader of the Israelites. Moses had blessed the people and had climbed Mount Nebo. There he died, looking over the Promised Land.

The river Jordan flowed between the Israelites and the Promised Land. The city of Jericho was on the other side, and the Israelites had to attack this city first. Spies were sent out to Jericho and they hid in the house of a woman called Rahab. The spies promised that her life would be saved when the Israelites attacked the city.

Joshua got his army ready. First, the priests carried the Ark of the Covenant through the river. When they stepped into the river, the water parted and they walked across dry land. The army followed, and then the waters closed up again.

Forty thousand soldiers now approached Jericho. The gates of the city were bolted tight. As Joshua looked toward the city, he saw a vision of a man standing in front of him with a sword. Joshua asked the man who he was. The man replied that he was the commander of the Lord's army. He told Joshua what he had to do to win the city.

The instructions God gave to Joshua were these. The army was to march around the city once a day for six days, with seven priests walking ahead of the Ark of the Covenant, and carrying trumpets made from ram's horns. On the seventh day, they were to march around the city seven times and then give loud blasts on the trumpets. All the people were to shout as loud as they could. And with this great noise the walls would come tumbling down.

That day, the army marched around the city once. The next day, they marched round again. The day after, and the day after that, they marched round again, until they had gone round the city every day for six days.

On the seventh day, they did as God commanded, and they marched round the city seven times. The priests blew loudly on their trumpets. Joshua told the people to shout, and they all shouted as loudly as they could. The walls of Jericho collapsed and crumbled! The army moved in and took the city. The gold and silver were saved, but everything else was destroyed. The promise the spies made to Rahab was kept. Joshua sent the men to search for her and save her. She was rescued along with her father, mother and other relatives.

You can find this story in Joshua chapters 1-6.

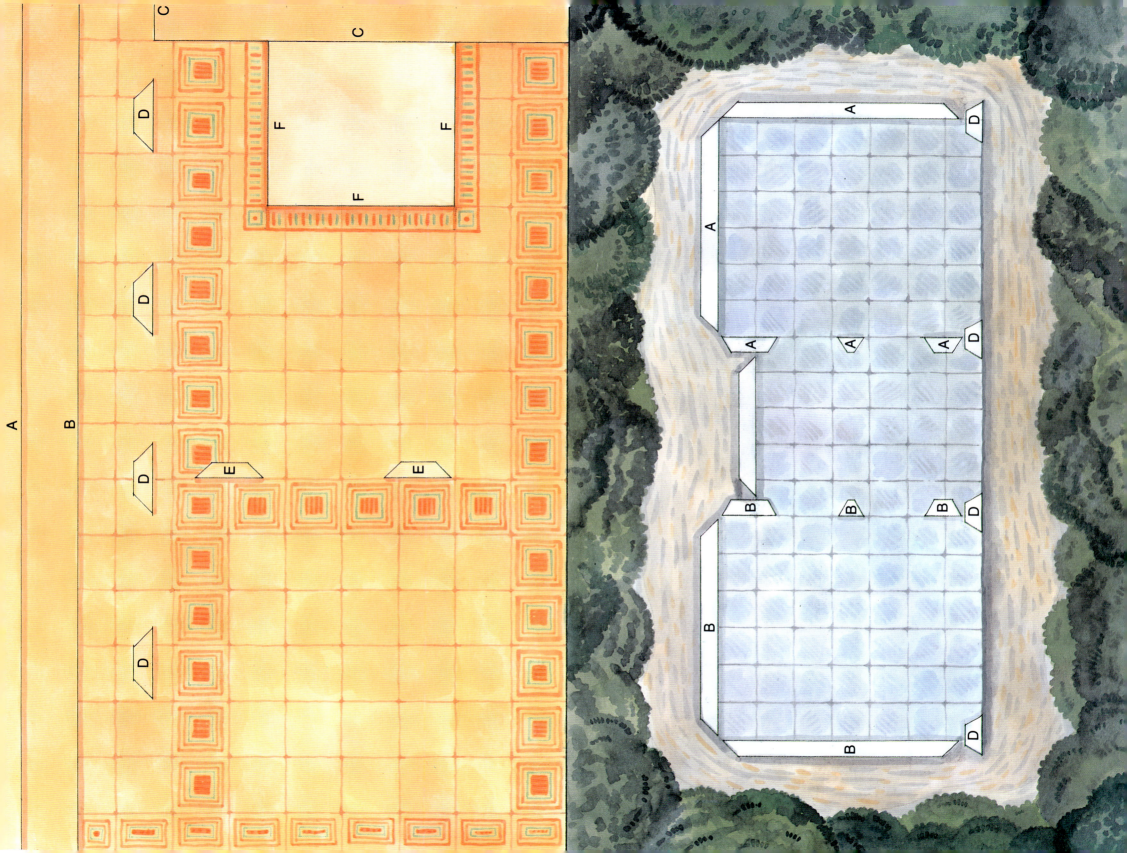

BASEBOARD
2

BASEBOARD
1

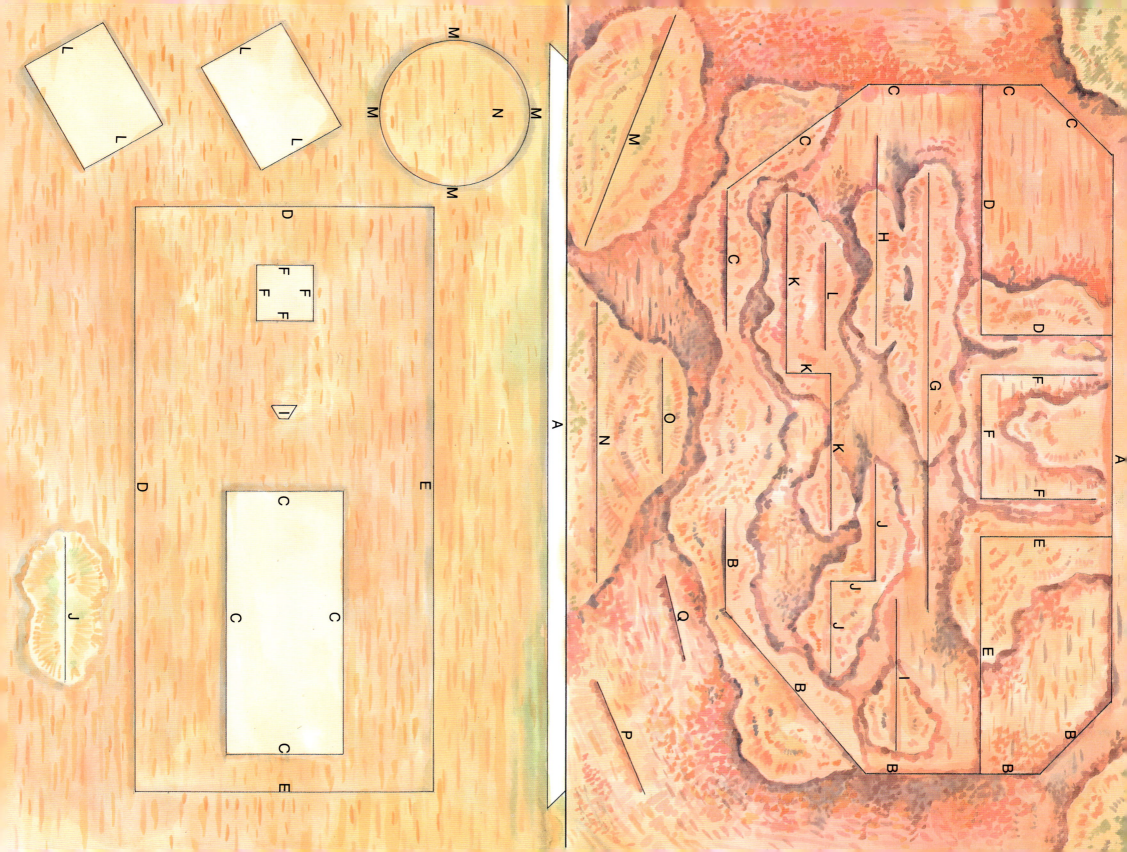

BASEBOARD
4

BASEBOARD
3

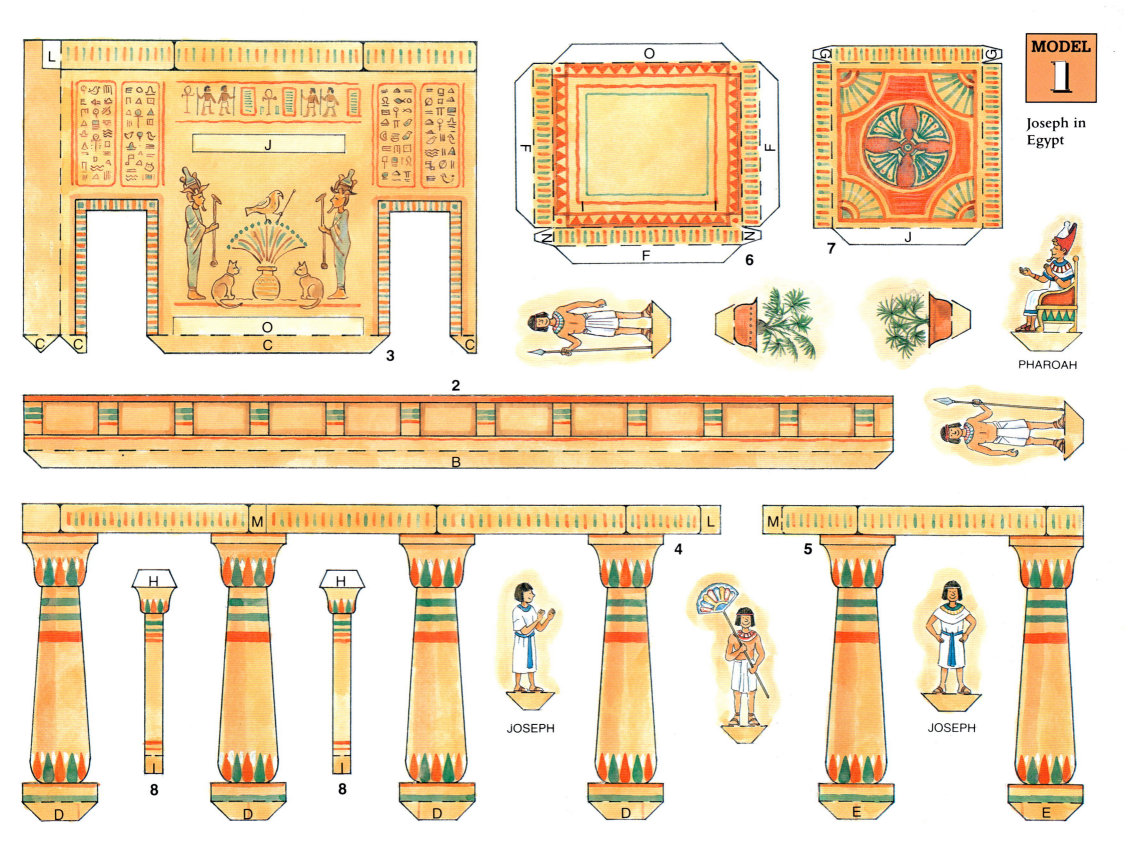

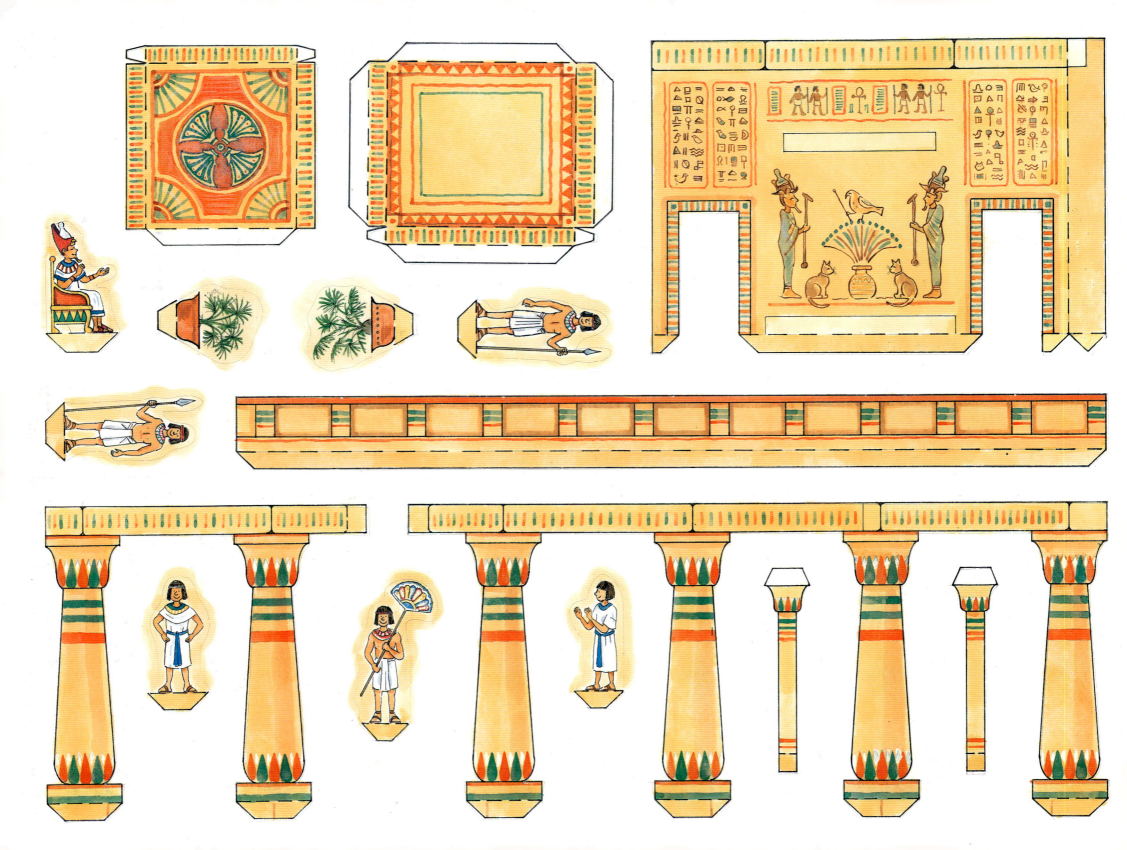

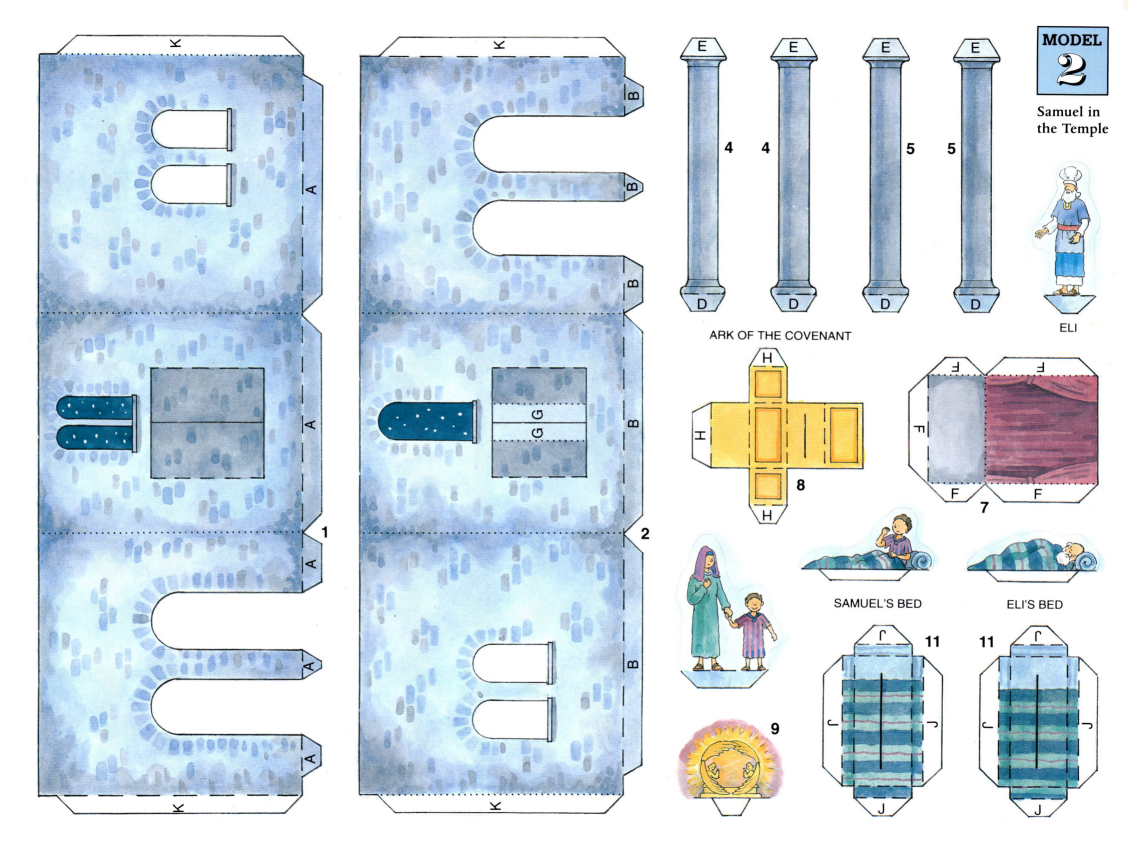

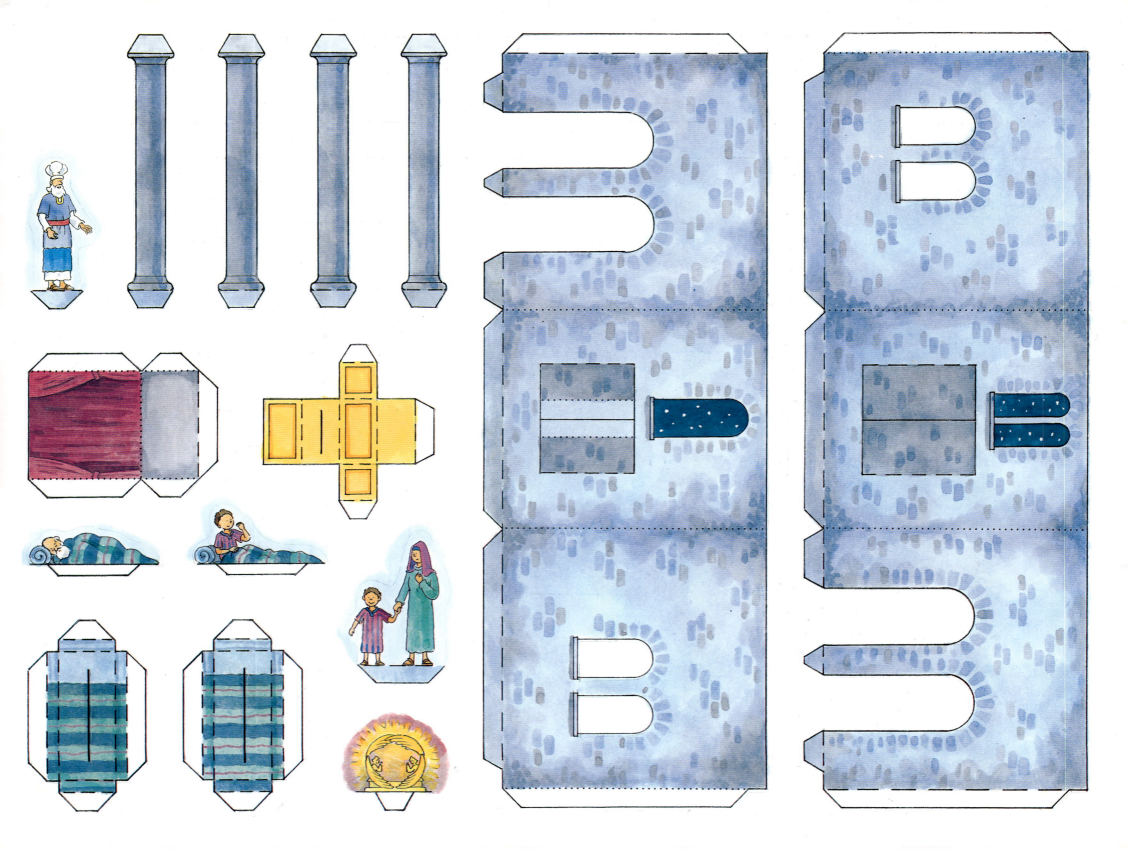

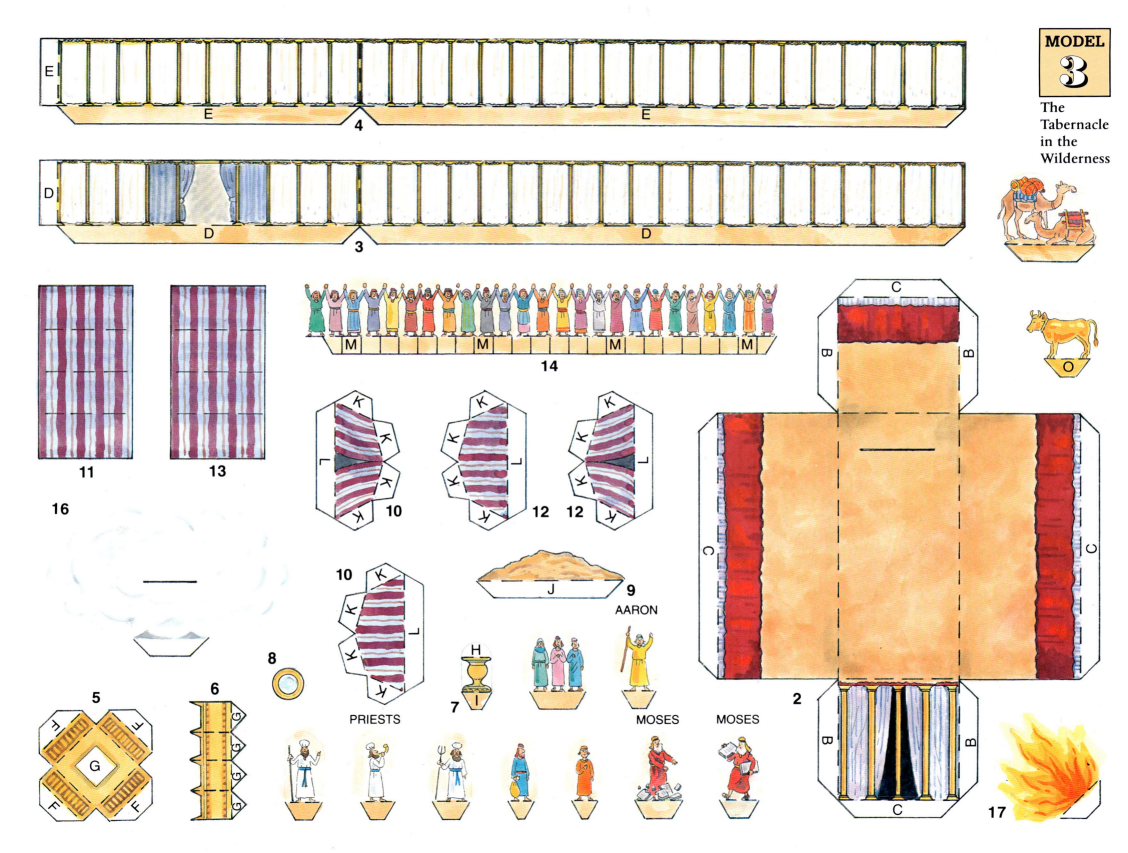

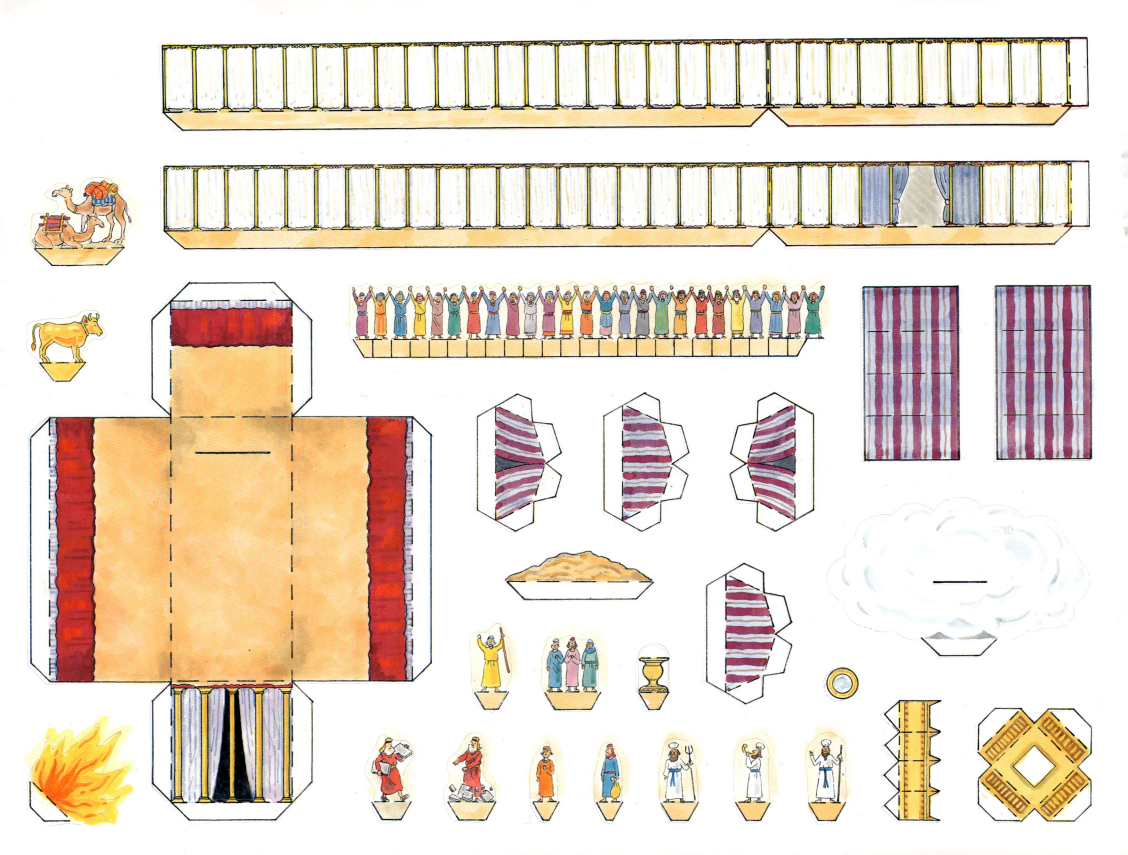

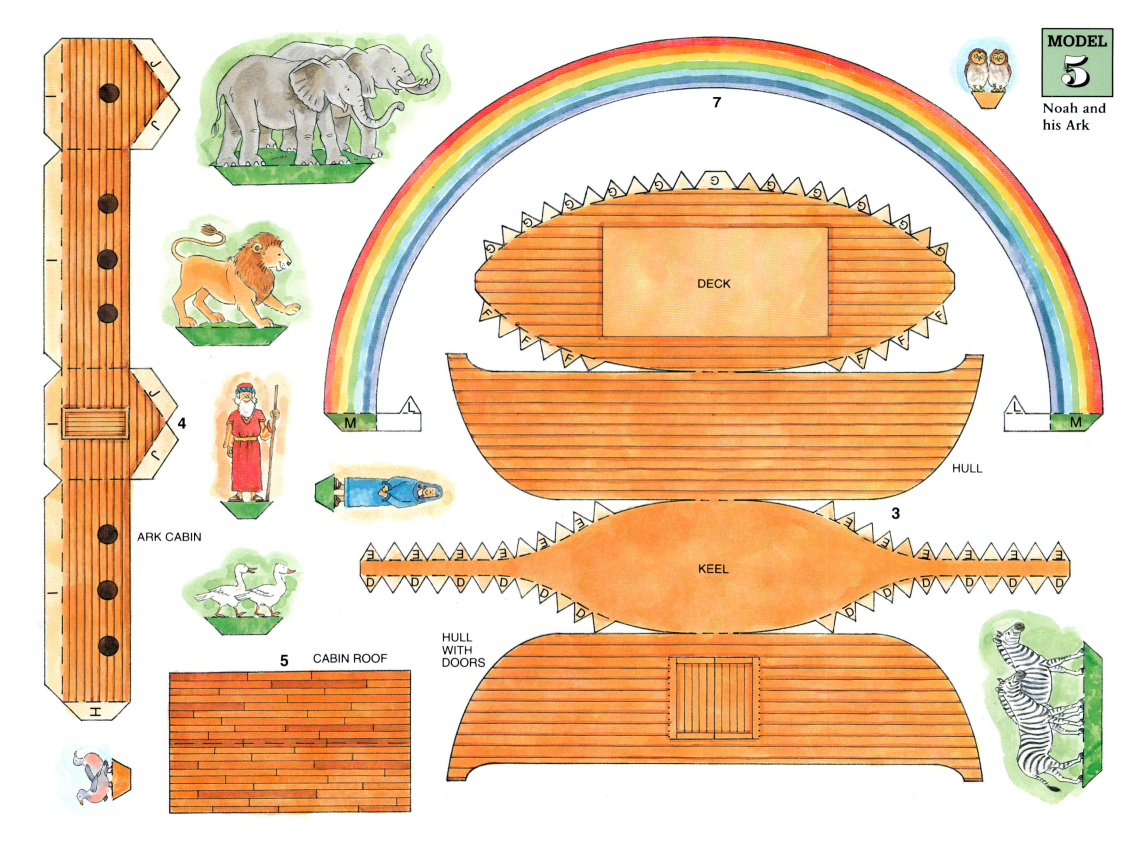

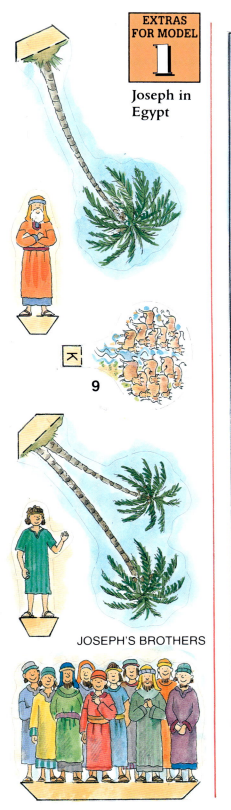
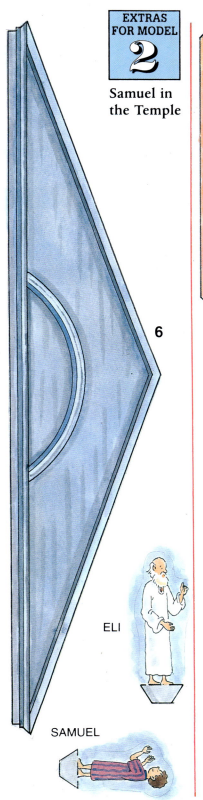
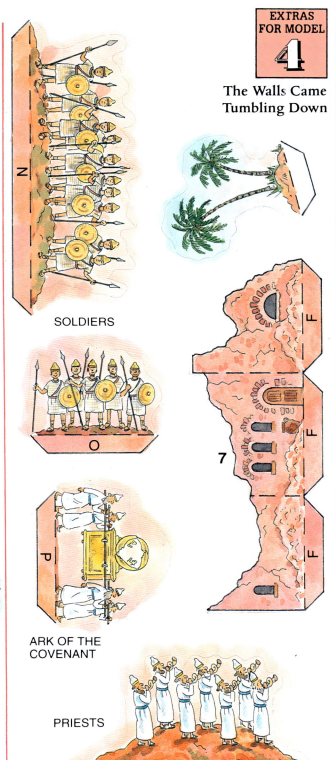
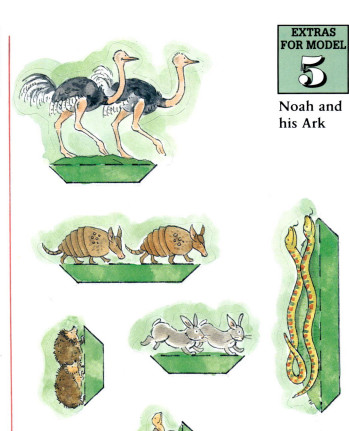

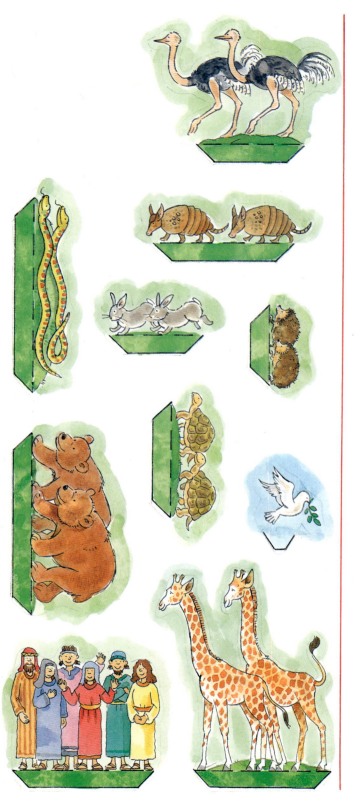

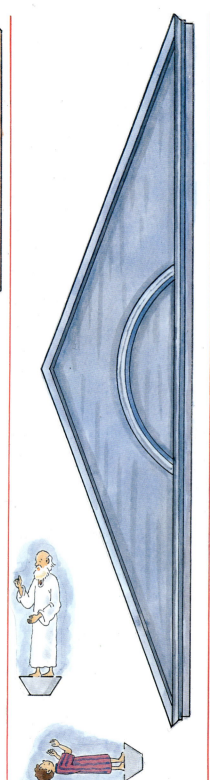
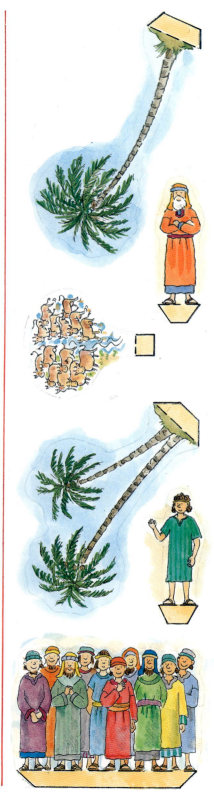

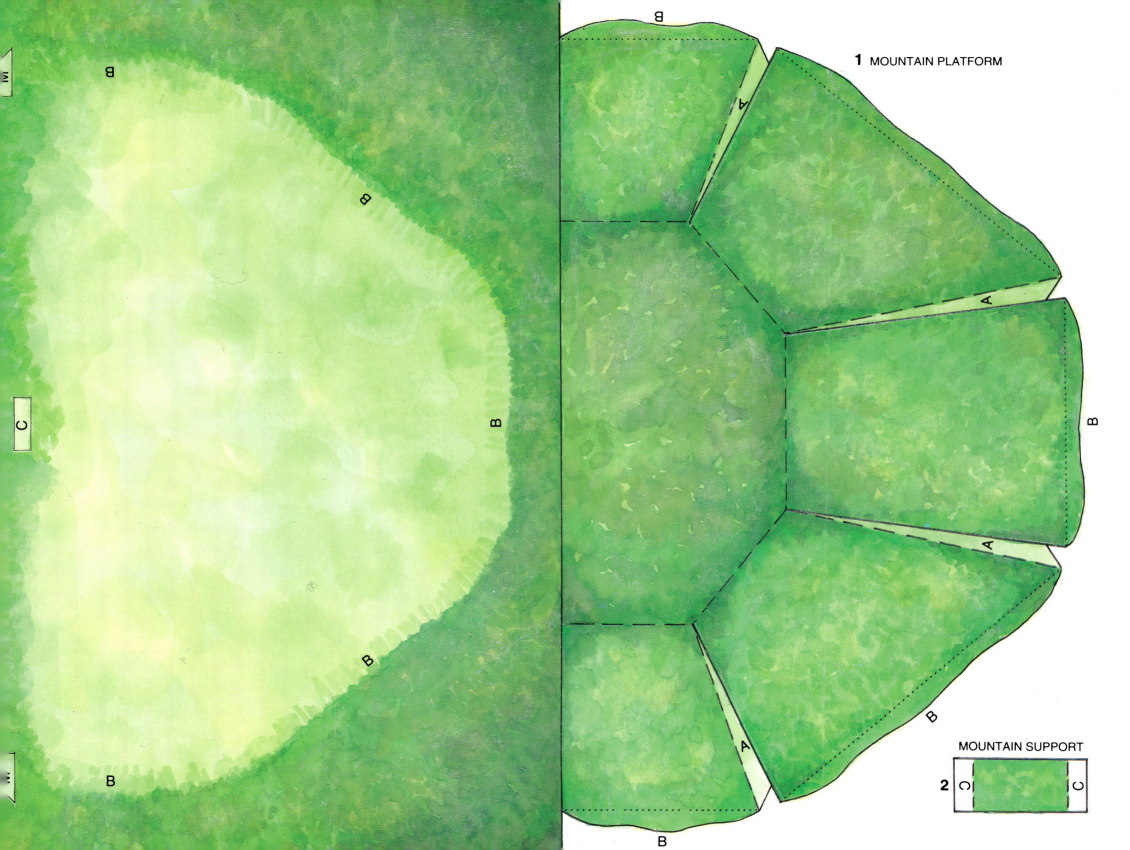

BASEBOARD
5

Noah and his Ark

STORY 5

Many, many years after God created the world, the number of people had greatly increased. Sadly, most of them were very wicked, except for one man. His name was Noah, and he was a farmer. He was also very clever at making things. More important though, was the fact that Noah was a good man and he loved God.

Things had got so bad that God decided to cause a great flood. Everything would be washed away so that there could be a new beginning.

God gave Noah very clear instructions on how to build a huge ship. Noah and his family would live in it when the flood came. God also told Noah to take two of every living creature into the ship as well.

People came from miles around to see the Ark being built. They laughed at Noah when he told them about the coming flood. When the Ark was ready Noah herded all the creatures into it. God closed the door, and they waited for the rain.

They did not have long to wait. It started with just a few drops and steadily got heavier and heavier until it was a real deluge. The water grew deeper around the boat until it began to float.

It rained for forty days and forty nights. For all that time, Noah and his family were busy looking after all the animals. At last, one day the rain stopped and everybody cheered. It took a long time for the water to go down, but when it did, the Ark was resting on top of a mountain. Noah sent out a raven, but it could not find any dry land and returned to the Ark. Then Noah sent out a dove which also came back to the Ark. Later, he sent out another dove, and this time it came back with a fresh olive twig.

Very soon after that, Noah opened the door of the Ark. All Noah's family rushed out and the animals followed. Noah and his family thanked God for saving them.

Then something remarkable happened. A beautiful rainbow appeared in the sky above them. God promised that he would never again destroy the earth with a flood, and the rainbow was a sign of this promise.

Remember this story the next time you see a rainbow.

You can find this story in Genesis chapters 6-9.

Instructions

MODEL 1
Joseph in Egypt

1. Cut out BASEBOARD **1**.
   Press out and fold WALL **3**.
   Glue tabs **C** and stick to the BASEBOARD.

2. Press out and fold PILLARS **4** and **5**.
   Glue tabs **D** and position on the BASEBOARD, sticking tab **L** to WALL **3**.

   Glue tabs **E** and stick to the BASEBOARD.
   Glue tab **M** and stick to **M** on PILLARS **4**. (Diagram 1).

3. Press out and fold THRONE BASE **6**. Glue tabs **N** in position.
   Glue tabs **F** to BASEBOARD and WALL **3**.
   Glue tabs **F** and stick to the BASEBOARD.
   Press out PHARAOH and stick him to the THRONE BASE.

4. Press out and fold THRONE CANOPY **7**.
   Glue tabs **G** and stick in position to form canopy.
   Press out and fold THRONE PILLARS **8**.
   Glue tabs **H** and stick inside the edge of the CANOPY, facing outwards.
   Glue tab **J** and tabs **I**. Stick them in position on the WALL and THRONE BASE. (Diagram 2).

5. Press out and fold DREAMS **9**.
   Glue tabs **K** and stick on top of the CANOPY.

6. Press out WALL **2**.
   Glue tab **B** and stick in position on the BASEBOARD.
   Press out the TREES for MODEL **1** and stick them in front of WALL **2**.
   Cut out BACKGROUND WITH PYRAMIDS **1**.
   Glue tab **A** and stick onto the BASEBOARD.

7. Read STORY **1** and position the people onto the BASEBOARD.

- All **diagrams** for these models are on the back page.

MODEL 2
Samuel in the Temple

1. Cut out BASEBOARD **2**.

2. Press out and fold WALLS **1** and PILLARS **4**.
   Glue PILLARS to tabs **K**. (Diagram 3).
   Glue tabs **A** and **D**.
   Stick in position on the BASEBOARD.

3. Cut out and fold WALL SECTION **3**.
   Glue tabs **C** and stick in position on BASEBOARD up against WALL **1**.

4. Press out and fold WALLS **2** and PILLARS **5**.
   Glue tabs **B** and **D**.
   Stick in position on the BASEBOARD, next to WALL **3**.

5. Cut out ROOF **6** and glue in position to tabs **E**.

6. Press out and fold NICHE **7**.
   Glue tabs **F** and stick in position at the back of WALL **1**. (Diagram 4).

7. Press out and fold ARK BOX.
   Glue tabs **H** and stick into a box shape.
   Press out ANGELS **9** and slot into top of ARK.
   Glue inside NICHE.

8. Cut out and fold SCROLLS **10**.
   Glue tabs **G** and position at the back of WALL **2**. (Diagram 5)

9. Press out and fold two BEDS **11**.
   Press out SAMUEL and ELI in bed and slot them into the BEDS.
   Glue tabs J and stick them onto the BASEBOARD in the positions marked.

10. Read STORY **2** and position the remaining figures onto the BASEBOARD.

Instructions

MODEL 3
The Tabernacle in the Wilderness

1. Cut out BASEBOARD 4 and MOUNT SINAI
   Fold tab **A** and glue into position on the BASEBOARD.

2. Press out and fold TENT TEMPLE 2.
   Glue tabs **B** and stick into a box shape. (Diagram 8).
   Glue tabs **C** and position onto the BASEBOARD.

3. Press out and fold ENCLOSURE 3.
   Glue tabs **D** and position to form two sides of the courtyard.
   Press out and fold ENCLOSURE 4.
   Glue tabs **E** and position on the BASEBOARD to complete the courtyard.

4. Press out and fold ALTAR BASE 5 and ALTAR 6.
   Glue tabs **F** and position onto BASEBOARD to form a plinth.
   Fold ALTAR 6 into a box shape, then glue tabs **G** and stick onto the BASE.

5. Press out LAVER BOWL parts 7 and 8.
   Fold tabs **H** and glue disc 8 on top of it.
   Glue tab **I** and position LAVER BOWL onto the BASEBOARD.

6. Press out and fold MOUND 9. Glue tab **J** to BASEBOARD.

7. Press out and fold TENT END 10 (two pieces) and TENT TOP 11.
   Take one of the TENT ENDS and glue tabs marked **K**.
   Stick the two pieces together and hold firmly until dry.
   Now glue the second TENT END in position. (Diagram 9).
   Repeat this with TENT ENDS 12 and TENT TOP 13.
   Glue tabs marked **L** on both tents and stick onto the BASEBOARD.

8. Press out DANCING PEOPLE 14 and form a ring.
   Glue all the tabs (some are marked **M**), and position onto the BASEBOARD.
   Cut out 15 and fold into a box.
   Glue tabs **N** to the BASEBOARD in centre of circle.
   Press out GOLDEN CALF **O** and glue on top of the box.

9. As you read STORY 4, position Moses on the mountain, and the other people onto the BASEBOARD.
   Slot CLOUD 16 and FIRE 17 into the top of the tabernacle.

MODEL 4
The Walls Came Tumbling Down

1. Cut out BASEBOARD 3 and MOUNTAIN 1.
   Glue MOUNTAIN to BASEBOARD.

2. Press out and fold WALL 2.
   Glue tab **A** and stick it on top of MOUNTAIN tab.
   Press out and fold 14 and glue tabs **R** between MOUNTAIN 1 and WALL 2.

3. Press out and fold WALL 3.
   Glue tabs **B** and stick in position on the BASEBOARD.
   Stick end tab to the back of WALL 2.
   Follow the guidelines on the BASEBOARD very carefully. (Diagram 6).

4. Press out, fold and glue WALL 4 in the same way as for WALL 3, to form the second city wall.

5. Press out and fold 5, 6 and 7. Glue them to the BASEBOARD following the guidelines.
   Make sure the end tabs on WALLS 5 and 6 are glued to WALLS 4 and 3.

6. Press out and fold WALLS 8, 9 and 10, then glue into position on the BASEBOARD.

7. Press out and fold WALLS 11 and 12.
   Glue onto the BASEBOARD, carefully following the zig-zag guidelines.

8. Cut and press out RUBBLE MOUNDS marked **L**.
   Cut out the PALM TREES.
   Glue these pieces onto the BASEBOARD. (See photograph for suggested positions).

9. Press out and fold SOLDIERS and PRIESTS with tabs marked **M**, **N**, **O**, **P**, and **Q**.
   Glue them into position on the BASEBOARD.

10. Carefully cut out and fold WALL 13.
    This is a removable section of the city wall, so do not glue in position – place it between parts 3 and 4. (Diagram 7).

Instructions

MODEL 5
Noah and his Ark

You may like to ask an adult for some help with this model as it is more complicated than the others

1. Cut out BASEBOARD 5 and MOUNTAIN PLATFORM 1.
   Cut along all **solid lines** (4 in all) on MOUNTAIN PLATFORM.
   Fold tabs **A** and base tabs **B**.
   Glue tabs **A** and stick them **under** the next segment of card.
   This will form the RAISED MOUNTAIN with a flat top. (Diagram 10)

2. Cut out and fold the MOUNTAIN SUPPORT 2.
   Glue **one** of the tabs marked C and stick it in position at the back of the BASEBOARD.
   Glue the other tab marked **C** and the underside of all tabs (**B**) around the base of the MOUNTAIN.
   Position the MOUNTAIN onto the BASEBOARD, making sure it is supported.

3. Press out and fold ARK 3. Open the ARK DOORS.
   Cut out RAMP 6.
   Glue the reverse side of the card, just beneath the ARK DOORS.
   Stick the RAMP in position with tab **K**, and hold firmly until dry. (Diagram 11).

4. Glue tabs **D** on KEEL along the inside edge of HULL WITH DOORS. Do this one end at a time, carefully following the curve of the HULL. (Diagram 12).
   (This stage is quite tricky, so take your time with it).
   Now repeat this process, gluing tabs **E** to the inside edge of the other part of the HULL.
   Hold until dry.

5. Fold DECK down and glue tabs **F** along the inside of the top edge of the HULL. Hold until dry.
   Glue tabs **G** and carefully pull HULL WITH DOORS out, so that tabs **G** can be stuck along the inside of the top edge to form the completed HULL. (Diagram 13).
   (It may help to push your finger through the ARK DOORS to hold the tabs in place until dry).

6. Press out and fold ARK CABIN 4.
   Glue tab **H** and form into a box shape. (Diagram 14).
   Glue tabs **I** and stick ARK CABIN onto the DECK.
   Press out ROOF 5. Glue tabs **J** on CABIN, then position the ROOF on top.

7. Press out and fold RAINBOW 7.
   Glue tabs **L** to the back of the RAINBOW to form a support. (Diagram 15).
   Glue tabs **M** and position onto BASEBOARD.

8. Glue the completed ARK in position on the MOUNTAIN.
   Cut and press out all the animals and people.
   Position them onto the ARK and the BASEBOARD as you read STORY 5.